The
COMPANIONS *in Christ*
Network

www.companionsinchrist.org

So much more!

Companions in Christ is *so much more* than printed resources.
It offers an ongoing LEADERSHIP NETWORK that provides:

➤ Opportunities to connect with other small groups who are also journeying through the *Companions in Christ* series.

➤ Insights and testimonies from other *Companions in Christ* participants

➤ An online discussion room where you can share or gather information

➤ Training opportunities that develop and deepen the leadership skills used in formational groups

➤ Helpful leadership tips and articles as well as updated lists of supplemental resources

Just complete this form and drop it in the mail, and you can enjoy the many benefits available through the *Companions in Christ* NETWORK! Or, enter your contact information at www.companionsinchrist.org/leaders.

Name: _____

Address: _____

City/State/Zip: _____

Church: _____

Email: _____

Phone: _____

COMPANIONS *in Christ*
Upper Room Ministries
PO Box 340012
Nashville, TN 37203-9540

COMPANIONS *in Christ*

A SMALL-GROUP EXPERIENCE IN SPIRITUAL FORMATION

FEEDING
~ on the WORD

Participant's Book   Volume 2

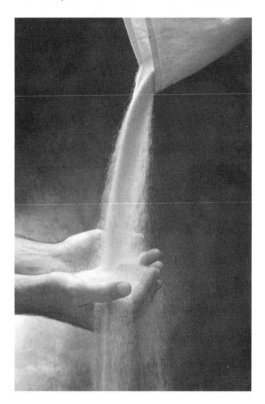

E. Glenn Hinson

UPPER ROOM BOOKS®
NASHVILLE

COMPANIONS IN CHRIST
FEEDING ON THE WORD: THE MIND OF CHRIST
Participant's Book: Part 2
Copyright © 2006 by Upper Room Books®
All rights reserved.

Cover design: Left Coast Design, Portland, OR
Cover photo: G. Biss; Masterfile
Interior icon development: Michael C. McGuire, settingPace
First printing: 2006

ISBN 0-8358-9831-8

Printed in the United States of America

For more information on *Companions in Christ*
call 800-972-0433 or visit www.companionsinchrist.org

Contents

Acknowledgments

Companions in Christ is truly the result of the efforts of a team of persons who shared a common vision. This team graciously contributed their knowledge and experience to develop a small-group resource that would creatively engage persons in a journey of spiritual growth and discovery. The author of Part 2 was E. Glenn Hinson. Stephen Bryant was the primary author of the daily exercises and the Leader's Guide. Marjorie Thompson created the original design and participated in the editing of the entire resource. Keith Beasley-Topliffe served as a consultant in the creation of the process for the small-group meetings and contributed numerous ideas that influenced the final shape of the resource. In the early stages of development, two advisory groups read and responded to the initial drafts of material. The persons participating as members of those advisory groups were Jeannette Bakke, Avery Brooke, Thomas Parker, Helen Pearson Smith, Luther E. Smith Jr., Eradio Valverde Jr., Diane Luton Blum, Carol Bumbalough, Ruth Torri, and Mark Wilson. Prior to publication, test groups in the following churches used the material and provided helpful suggestions for improvement of the Participant's Books and the Leader's Guide.

First United Methodist Church, Hartselle, Alabama
St. George's Episcopal Church, Nashville, Tennessee

Acknowledgments

Northwest Presbyterian Church, Atlanta, Georgia
Garfield Memorial United Methodist Church,
    Pepper Pike, Ohio
First United Methodist Church, Corpus Christi, Texas
Malibu United Methodist Church, Malibu, California
First United Methodist Church, Santa Monica, California
St. Paul United Methodist Church, San Antonio, Texas
Trinity Presbyterian Church, Arvada, Colorado
First United Methodist Church, Franklin, Tennessee
La Trinidad United Methodist Church, San Antonio, Texas
Aldersgate United Methodist Church, Slidell, Louisiana

My deep gratitude goes to all these persons and groups for their contribution to and support of *Companions in Christ*.

—Janice T. Grana, editor of *Companions in Christ*
April 2001

Introduction

Welcome to Part 2 of *Companions in Christ*, a small-group resource for spiritual formation designed to create a setting where you can respond to God's call to an ever-deepening communion and wholeness in Christ—as an individual, as a member of a small group, and as part of a congregation. The resource focuses on your experience of God and your discovery of spiritual practices that help you share more fully in the life of Christ. You will be exploring the potential of Christian community as an environment of grace and mutual guidance through the Spirit. You will grow closer to members of your small group as you seek together to know and respond to God's will. And your congregation will grow when you and your companions begin to bring what you learn into all areas of church life, from classes and meetings to worship and outreach.

How does *Companions in Christ* help you grow spiritually? It enables you to immerse yourself in "streams of living waters" through the spiritual disciplines of prayer, scripture, ministry, worship, study, and Christian conversation. These means of grace are the common ways in which Christ meets people, renews their faith, and deepens their life together in love.

In the previous part, "Embracing the Journey," you were introduced to spiritual formation as a journey. In Part 2, you will explore the depths of scripture, learn to listen to God through it, and allow your life to be shaped by the Word.

In the remaining three units:

- You will experience new dimensions of prayer, try fresh ways of opening to God, and learn what it means to practice the presence of God.

- You will reflect on Christ's call in your life and discover anew the gifts that God is giving you for living out your personal ministry.

- You and members of your group will grow together as a Christian community and gain skills in learning how small groups in the church become settings for spiritual guidance.

Although *Companions* is not an introductory course in Christianity for new Christians, it will help church people take up the basic disciplines of faith in renewing and transforming ways.

An Outline of the Resource

Companions in Christ has two primary components: individual reading and daily exercises throughout the week with this Participant's Book and a weekly two-hour meeting based on suggestions in the Leader's Guide. For each week, the Participant's Book has a chapter introducing new material and five daily exercises to help you reflect on your life in light of the content of the chapter. After the Preparatory Meeting of your group, you will begin a weekly cycle as follows: On day 1 you will be asked to read the chapter and on days 2–6 to complete the five daily exercises (found at the end of the chapter reading). On day 7 you will meet with your group. The daily exercises aim to help you move from information (knowledge about) to experience (knowledge of). An important part of this process is keeping a personal notebook or journal where you record reflections, prayers, and questions for later review and for reference at the weekly group meeting. The time commitment for the daily exercises is about thirty minutes. The weekly meeting will include time for reflecting on the exercises of the past week, for moving deeper into learnings from chapter readings, for having group experiences of prayer, and for considering ways to share with the congregation what you have learned or experienced.

The complete material in *Companions in Christ* covers a period of twenty-eight weeks divided into five parts or units, of which this volume is the second. The five parts are as follows:

1. *Embracing the Journey: The Way of Christ* (five weeks)—a basic exploration of spiritual formation as a journey toward wholeness and holiness, individually and in community, through the grace of God.

2. *Feeding on the Word: The Mind of Christ* (five weeks)—an introduction to several ways of meditating on and praying with scripture.

3. *Deepening Our Prayer: The Heart of Christ* (six weeks)—a guided experience of various forms and styles of prayer.

4. *Responding to Our Call: The Work of Christ* (five weeks)—a presentation of vocation or call: giving ourselves to God in willing obedience and receiving the fruits and gifts of the Holy Spirit.

5. *Exploring Spiritual Guidance: The Spirit of Christ* (five weeks)—an overview of different ways of giving and receiving spiritual guidance, from one-on-one relationships, to spiritual growth groups, to guidance in congregational life as a whole.

Your group may want to take a short break between units either to allow for some unstructured reflection time or to avoid meeting near Christmas or Easter. However, the units are designed to be sequential—each unit builds on previous ones.

This Participant's Book includes a section titled "Materials for Group Meetings." This section includes some brief supplemental readings that you will use as a part of one or more group meetings. Your leader will alert you when you will be using this material. Also you will find an annotated resource list that describes additional books related to the theme of this part of *Companions in Christ*.

You will need to bring your Participant's Book, your Bible, and your personal notebook or journal to the weekly group meeting.

The Companions in Christ Network

An additional dimension of *Companions in Christ* is the Network. While you and your group are experiencing *Companions in Christ*, groups in other congregations will also be meeting. The Network provides opportunities for you to share your experiences with one another and to link in a variety of meaningful ways. As you move through the resource, there will be occasions when you will be invited to pray for another group, send greetings or encouragement, or receive their support for your group. Connecting in these ways will enrich your group's experience and the experience of those to whom you reach out.

The Network also provides a place to share conversation and information. The Companion's Web site, www.companionsinchrist.org, includes a discussion room where you can offer insights, voice questions, and respond to others in an ongoing process of shared learning. The site provides a list of other Companions groups and their geographical locations so that you can make connections as you feel led.

The Companions Network is a versatile and dynamic component of the larger *Companions* resource. A Network toll-free number (1-800-972-0433) is staffed during regular business hours to take your order.

Your Personal Notebook or Journal

"I began these pages for myself, in order to think out my own particular pattern of living. . . . And since I think best with a pencil in my hand, I started naturally to write." Anne Morrow Lindbergh began her beloved classic, *Gift from the Sea*, with these words. You may not imagine that you "think best with a pencil in hand," but there is something truly wonderful about what can happen when we reflect on the inner life through writing.

Keeping a journal or personal notebook (commonly called journaling) will be one of the most important dimensions of your personal experience with *Companions in Christ*. The Participant's Book gives you daily spiritual exercises every week. More often than not, you will be asked to note your thoughts, reflections, questions, feelings, or prayers in relation to the exercises.

Even if you are totally inexperienced in this kind of personal writing, you may find that it becomes second nature very quickly. Your thoughts may start to pour out of you, giving expression to an inner life that has never been released. If, on the other hand, you find the writing difficult or cumbersome, give yourself permission to try it in a new way. Because a journal is "for your eyes only," you may choose any style that suits you. You need not worry about making your words sound beautiful or about writing with good grammar and spelling. You don't even need to write complete sentences! Jotting down key ideas, insights, or musings is just fine. You might want to doodle while you think or sketch an image that comes to you. Make journaling fun and relaxed. No one will see what you write, and you have complete freedom to share with the group only what you choose of your reflections.

There are two important reasons for keeping a journal or personal notebook as you move through *Companions in Christ*. First, the process of writing down our thoughts clarifies them for us. They become more specific and concrete. Sometimes we really do not know what we think until we see our thoughts on paper, and often the process of writing itself generates new creative insight. Second, this personal record captures what we have been experiencing inwardly over time. Journaling helps us track changes in our thinking and growth of insight. Our memories are notoriously fragile and fleeting in this regard. Specific feelings or creative connections we may have had two weeks ago, or even three days ago, are hard to recall without a written record. Even though your journal cannot capture all that goes through your mind in a single reflection period, it will serve as a reminder. You will need to draw on these reminders during small-group meetings each week.

Begin by purchasing a book that you can use for this purpose. It can be as simple as a spiral-bound notebook or as fancy as a cloth-bound blank book. Some people prefer lined paper and some unlined. You will want, at minimum, something more permanent than a ring-binder or paper pad. The Upper Room has made available a companion journal for this resource that you can purchase if you so desire. Or you can use the blank pages at the back of this book.

When you begin the daily exercises, have your journal and pen or pencil at hand. You need not wait until you have finished reading and thinking an exercise through completely. Learn to stop and write as you go. Think on paper. Feel free to write anything that comes to you, even if it seems to be "off the topic." It may turn out to be more relevant or useful than you first think. If the process seems clumsy at first, don't fret. Like any spiritual practice, it gets easier over time, and its value becomes more apparent.

Here is how your weekly practice of journaling is shaped. On the first day after your group meeting, read the new chapter. Jot down your responses to the reading: "aha" moments, questions, points of disagreement, images, or any other reflections you wish to record. You may prefer to note these in the margins of the chapter. Over the next five days, you will do the exercises for the week, recording either general or specific responses as they are invited. On the day of the group meeting, it will be helpful to review what you have written through the week, perhaps marking portions you would like to share in the group. Bring your journal with you to meetings so that you can refer to it directly or refresh your memory of significant moments you want to paraphrase during discussion times. With time, you may indeed find that journaling helps you to think out your own pattern of living and that you will be able to see more clearly how God is at work in your life.

Your Group Meeting

The weekly group meeting is divided into four segments. First you will gather for a brief time of worship and prayer. This offers an opportunity to set aside the many concerns of the day and center on God's presence and guidance as you begin your group session.

The second section of the meeting is called "Sharing Insights."

During this time you will be invited to talk about your experiences with the daily exercises. The group leader will participate as a member and share his or her responses as well. Generally the sharing by each member will be brief and related to specific exercises. This is an important time for your group to learn and practice what it means to be a community of persons seeking to listen to God and to live more faithfully as disciples of Christ. The group provides a supportive space to explore your listening, your spiritual practices, and how you are attempting to put those practices into daily life. Group members need not comment or offer advice to one another. Rather the group members help you, by their attentiveness and prayer, to pay attention to what has been happening in your particular response to the daily exercises. The group is not functioning as a traditional support group that offers suggestions or help to one another. Rather, the group members trust that the Holy Spirit is the guide and that they are called to help one another listen to that guidance.

The "Sharing Insights" time presents a unique opportunity to learn how God works differently in each of our lives. Our journeys, while varied, are enriched by others' experiences. We can hold one another in prayer, and we can honor each other's experience. Through this part of the meeting, you will see in fresh ways how God's activity may touch or address our lives in unexpected ways. The group will need to establish some ground rules to facilitate the sharing. For example, you may want to be clear that each person speak only about his or her own beliefs, feelings, and responses and that all group members have permission to share only what and when they are ready to share. Above all, the group needs to maintain confidentiality so that what is shared in the group stays in the group. This part of the group meeting will be much less meaningful if persons interrupt and try to comment on what is being said or try to "fix" what they see as a problem. The leader will close this part of the meeting by calling attention to any patterns or themes that seem to emerge from the group's sharing. These patterns may point to a word that God is offering to the group. Notice that the group leader functions both as a participant and as someone who aids the process by listening and summarizing the key insights that have surfaced.

The third segment of the group meeting is called "Deeper Explorations." This part of the meeting may expand on ideas contained in the week's chapter, offer practice in the spiritual disciplines introduced in the chapter or exercises, or give group members a chance to reflect on the implications of what they are learning for themselves and for their church. It offers a common learning experience for the group and a chance to go deeper in our understanding of how we can share more fully in the mind, heart, and work of Jesus Christ.

As it began, the group meeting ends with a brief time of worship, an ideal time for the group to share special requests for intercession that might come from the conversation and experience of the meeting or other prayer requests that arise naturally from the group.

The weeks that you participate in *Companions in Christ* will offer you the opportunity to focus on your relationship with Christ and to grow in your openness to God's presence and guidance. The unique aspect of this experience is that members of your small group, who are indeed your companions on the journey, will encourage your searching and learning. Those of us who have written and edited this resource offer our prayers that God will speak to you during these weeks and awaken you to enlarged possibilities of love and service in Christ's name. As we listen and explore together, we will surely meet our loving God who waits eagerly to guide us toward deeper maturity in Christ by the gracious working of the Holy Spirit.

Part 2

Feeding on the Word: The Mind of Christ

E. Glenn Hinson

Why Do We Call the Bible God's Word?

My grandmother left me my earliest memories of this fascinating book, the Bible. I can still see her sitting on the porch in her rocking chair, rocking back and forth, Bible open on her lap. Sometimes she went to sleep. But more often than not, I remember seeing tears dripping down onto the pages of her well-worn and well-marked Bible. I often asked her what was wrong. She usually replied, "Shh! I'm just seeking a word from God."

As a four- or five-year-old, I got my first personal exposure to the Bible in a Lutheran Sunday school in St. Louis, Missouri. A teacher told us Bible stories, and we colored pictures illustrating them. Born into a family of conflict with already painful memories, I found some heroes in those stories—Joseph, Moses, David, Jesus. I could scarcely wait to read the Bible for myself. In the sixty some years since then, I've read it many times. Well, I must confess that I have fudged a bit on the Baptist counsel to read straight through. Not once have I made it through Leviticus in that way.

Perhaps you have been drawn to the Bible but, apart from the structure of a church school class, you may have felt that it was difficult to understand and relate the Bible to your daily experience. You may have become confused by what seemed to be contradictions in the Bible. Or perhaps you have wanted to establish a pattern of daily

If you want true knowledge of the Scriptures, try to secure steadfast humility of heart, to carry you by the perfection of love not to knowledge that puffs up, but that enlightens.

—John Cassian

scripture reading but found that other activities continually usurped the time. In thinking together about the Bible as God's Word to us, I invite you to examine your attitudes toward scripture and your patterns of reading it. Prayer and Bible reading are deeply interwoven and offer us a discipline to listen to and meet the God who loves us.

How the Bible Came to Be

What a fascinating book the Bible is! Actually, to make it more intriguing still, I've had to recognize that it is not one book but many. It consists of different kinds of writings composed over several centuries and collected little by little, first by the Jewish people and later by Christians. The Hebrew Bible, what Christians have commonly referred to as the Old Testament, consists of accounts of the history of the Jewish people, stories of saints (Ruth, Esther), a masterpiece on human suffering (Job), a collection of songs (Psalms), an anthology of proverbs (Proverbs and Ecclesiastes), a narrative of a love tryst of newlyweds (Song of Solomon), and writings of prophets.

The Christian scriptures (the New Testament) are composed of four accounts of the story of Jesus (Gospels), an account of the early spread of Christianity (Acts of the Apostles), letters of Paul and other apostles, an early Christian sermon (Hebrews), and an apocalypse (Revelation). Until the Reformation of the sixteenth century and among Roman Catholics even today, the Christian scriptures have also included a group of writings called the Apocrypha. The Protestant reformers excluded them from their scriptures because they lacked Hebrew originals and did not belong to the Jewish canon. Today, however, many Protestant Bibles include the Apocrypha.

Given such diversity and time span, you may wonder how the Bible came to be. Obviously, its formation came in several stages. Stage one involved an oral account, for instance, of the exodus of the Hebrew people from Egypt and of the ministry, death, and resurrection of Jesus. Ancient peoples relied far more on memory than we do today. After a considerable period of time, certain people began to write down the stories people told, the songs they sang, the proverbs they quoted.

Stage two thus had to do with writing. Modern scholarship has shown that this was not a simple process with only one author composing one writing. In the case of the historical books, for instance, scholars have discerned the hands of several editors and revisers to produce writings such as the first few books of the Bible as they now stand. In the case of the Gospels we can see that both Matthew and Luke used Mark and another "source" in composing their accounts of the good news. Luke, in fact, speaks about "many" before him, who had "undertaken to set down an orderly account of the events that have been fulfilled among us" (Luke 1:1).

Stage three entailed reproduction and transmission. In the biblical period people did not have printing presses that could make this a simple task. They copied manuscripts by hand and circulated them to people who would read them. They could set up a copy business in which several scribes recorded what another person read, but as you would guess, handmade manuscripts cost dearly and did not circulate widely.

Stage four concerned the authoritative use of certain writings. The Hebrew people, for instance, did not immediately recognize the worth of a prophet like Jeremiah. Indeed, as he complained, some contemporaries laughed at him, denounced him, and reproached him when he spoke (Jer. 20:7-10). Only later did others see that he spoke the truth. They put his prophecies in a special category, reading them in public worship. Christian communities always considered the Old Testament authoritative, just as Jews did. Little by little, different churches singled out Christian writings they knew for use in public worship. Rome, for example, probably used Mark's Gospel; Antioch used Matthew's; Corinth used some of Paul's letters to them. In time collections of writings were recognized as authoritative (canonical), at first small ones and later larger ones.

Stage five involved the forming of authoritative collections on a wider scale. For the Old Testament we can see three blocks: the Law (the first five books), recognized as authoritative by around 400 B.C.E.; the Prophets (including some historical writings), by 150 B.C.E.; and the Writings (the rest of the Hebrew scriptures), not until rabbis

acknowledged them in meetings at the rabbinic school at Jamnia around 100 C.E. Degree of authority varied too. The Law stood well above the Prophets and other Writings.

Although the first Christians recognized the Hebrew Scriptures as their Bible too, by the second century C.E. they were ranking Christian writings alongside them. The four Gospels, the letters that went under Paul's name, First Peter, and First John quickly attained authoritative status in most churches. Other writings now in the New Testament were used in public worship in some churches but not in others. What most Christians would recognize today as the New Testament canon of twenty-seven books was not decided until the end of the fourth century in councils held at Carthage in North Africa.

The final stage is translation and circulation. Old Testament writings were composed mostly in Hebrew with a few Aramaic passages; the New Testament was written in the popular (*koine*) Greek, which was used commercially throughout the Roman Empire when Christianity came on the scene in the first century C.E. As an intensely missionary faith, Christianity soon translated both Hebrew and Christian scriptures into the dozens of popular languages of peoples who lived in or near the Roman Empire—such as Latin, Coptic (for Egypt), Armenian, and others. This stage continues even today.

The Relationship between the Hebrew and the Christian Scriptures

What is the relationship between the Hebrew and the Christian Scriptures? Christians have given different answers to that question. Although Christianity began as a sect of Judaism, by the late first century the child separated from the parent. The Christian Scriptures, however, raise here a very urgent question: How can they be understood unless we see the integral connection they have with the Hebrew Scriptures? The answer is, they cannot be. They are filled with citations and allusions from the Hebrew Scriptures and arguments based on them. The earliest Christians obviously lived by the Hebrew Scriptures just as Jesus and other Jews did. Consequently, Christians are

bound to keep the two sets of scriptures inseparably linked to each other. The Jewish people can live out of the Hebrew Scriptures as they have down through the centuries, but Christians cannot find their path using only Christian Scriptures. By themselves their scriptures will not be intelligible or speak with authority.

Responding to the Bible as God's Word

Both Jews and Christians have referred to this compilation of writings as the Word of God. What do they mean? Some contend that the scriptures are the Word of God in the sense that every syllable is inspired and therefore free from human error and infallible. They believe that God, the Holy Spirit, guided each author to write exactly what God intended.

Naturally, many others have not agreed with this theory of direct verbal inspiration. As an alternative, they believe that the Word of God is revelation, God's self-disclosure. The scriptures contain revelation, but not every word within them is that revelation. They believe God did not dictate the writings but, through the Holy Spirit, enabled human beings to discern God acting in nature, history, and the ordinary affairs of human life. The scriptures are thus the Word of God in the sense that they record God's self-disclosure in these ways. Scripture is also the Word of God in that, through its words, God searches, invites, challenges, and comforts us. Through the Bible, we hear God speaking a personal word to us.

When we refer to the Bible as the Word of God, we recognize the authority of scripture for our faith and practice. Scripture presents a living portrait of God and God's will for human beings. As such, it carries authority. To be quite honest, we human beings struggle to yield ourselves to that authority. Our pride often prevails. There is a sense in which the scriptures do not become the Word of God until we take them into our hearts and live the message they have for us. In recognition of the complex process by which that may happen, one church that I know follows the Sunday readings with the statement: "May these words become to us the Word of God."

Our own curiosity often hinders us in reading the Scriptures, because we wish to understand and argue when we should simply read on with humility, simplicity and faith.

—Thomas à Kempis

Where the Spirit does not open the Scripture, the Scripture is not understood even though it is read.

—Martin Luther

Here is where the Holy Spirit must come to our aid. The Spirit illumined minds to see what God was disclosing in nature, history, and human experience. The Spirit guided the complicated process of forming the collections of scriptures. Now the Holy Spirit must help us interpret and apply the Word of God. As Paul reminded the Romans with reference to prayer, "the Spirit helps us in our weakness" (Rom. 8:26). The Spirit searches our hearts, clarifies our understanding, and further directs us in our effort to apply biblical insights to everyday life. The Spirit also enables us to yield our wills to God's will, enticing and inspiring us to obedience. The Spirit gives vitality to the Word of God that, as the author of Hebrews concluded, "is living and active, sharper than any two-edged sword, piercing until it divides soul from spirit, joints from marrow" and "is able to judge the thoughts and intentions of the heart" (Heb. 4:12).

God's Word will speak to us and transform our lives if we will come to it in a spirit of prayer and expectancy. The invitation is for us to seek the living presence of God in the Bible and to come ready to listen and respond. When we read the scriptures with openness and trust, we will not be disappointed. Thomas Merton, a profound and influential writer of the twentieth century, reminds us that we will know and experience the Bible as God's Word because it will change and liberate our lives. He writes, "The 'word of God' is recognized in actual experience because it does something to anyone who really 'hears' it: it transforms his [or her] entire existence."[1]

DAILY EXERCISES

Be sure to read the chapter before you begin these exercises. Keep a journal or blank book beside you to record your thoughts, questions, prayers, and images. In preparation, quiet yourself and reflect on the following quotation by Robert Mulholland:

> Christian spiritual formation is the process of being conformed to the image of Christ. . . . The scripture stands close to the center of this whole process of being conformed to the image of Christ. As we shall see, the scripture is one of the primary channels through which God encounters us . . . and awakens us to the dynamics and possibilities of a new way of being.[2]

EXERCISE 1

Read Psalm 119:97-105. What is your favorite Bible story or scripture passage? Reflect on why and how you came to cherish it. Identify any special role it has played in your life, its meaning for you, and how God has spoken to you through it.

EXERCISE 2

Read Genesis 1. Again and again we read, "And God said. . . . And it was so." Our words and actions do not always correspond, but God's word and action are one and the same. What God speaks becomes reality—if not immediately, then eventually. Keeping this in mind, reread 1:26-31. Contemplate the promise of opening wide your life to the Word: "And God said. . . . And it was so." What could happen? Record your reflections in your journal.

EXERCISE 3

Read Psalm 1. This psalm was placed at the beginning of the Psalter to be a preface and to convey a promise: those who study God's law and live by God's Word will be "like trees planted by streams of water." Sketch a picture of two trees—one on each side of a page. Make one tree a depiction of your life as it is. Make the second tree a depiction of your life as it could be. Beneath and between the trees, list or write

out two or three passages of scripture that have been for you streams of nourishment and growth. Spend a few moments quietly reflecting on what God is saying to you. Capture your thoughts in writing.

EXERCISE 4

Read John 1:1-18. The prologue to John's Gospel makes the remarkable claim that the Word of God is not limited to words and letters in a book, but that "the Word became flesh and lived among us" in Jesus Christ. When have you seen Christ as living Word? What is the promise of receiving the "Word made flesh"? How could this revelation change the meaning of Bible "study"? Record your reflections in your journal.

EXERCISE 5

Read 2 Corinthians 3:1-6. The Apostle Paul, being a proficient letter writer, calls his faithful disciples "a letter of Christ, prepared by us, written not with ink but with the Spirit of the living God . . . on tablets of human hearts." What a commendation! Think about your life as a letter that you write with your words, attitudes, and actions. What does your "letter"—this week's letter—say or not say about Christ and his life in you? What word from Christ would the Spirit like to write on the tablet of your heart for all to read? Record your thoughts and offer them to God.

Remember to review your journal entries for the week in preparation for the group meeting.

Studying Scripture As a Spiritual Discipline

F or the words of scripture to become the Word of God we will need to use our minds to hear what God is saying to us. This involves serious attention to and study of scripture. The English word *study* derives from the Latin word *studere*, "to busy or apply oneself." Its contemporary definition is "the act or process of applying the mind in order to acquire knowledge" or "careful attention to, and critical examination and investigation of, any subject, event, etc." It especially involves the intellect, faith seeking understanding through the body of writings that contain testimonies to God's self-disclosure in nature, events, and persons.

Study as Essential to Understanding

Through the centuries the faithful have recognized that spiritual growth requires disciplined and steadfast attention to scripture. During the period of the Exile (589–20 B.C.E.) and after, as the Law increased in importance, skilled students and interpreters of the Law called scribes arose to lead the way in the study of scriptures.[1] In Jesus' day Jewish religious leaders searched the scriptures because they believed "that in them you have eternal life" (John 5:39).

The first Christians recognized how essential it was to apply their minds to scripture. For one thing, convincing those who lived in a

It is the duty of all Christians diligently to search the scriptures. . . . How useful soever this book of books is in itself, it will be of no use to us if we do not acquaint ourselves with it, by reading it daily, and meditating upon it, that we may understand the mind of God in it, and may apply what we understand to ourselves for our direction, rebuke, and comfort, as there is occasion.

—Matthew Henry

We will only be happy in our reading of the Bible when we dare to approach it as the means by which God really speaks to us, the God who loves us and will not leave us with our questions unanswered.

—Dietrich Bonhoeffer

Jewish context of the truth of their message required it. Luke paints a graphic picture of the application of the mind to scripture in his story of Philip's assisting the Ethiopian eunuch. "Do you understand what you are reading?" Philip asked. The eunuch replied, "How can I, unless someone guides me?" This exchange opened the way for Philip to proclaim the "good news about Jesus" (Acts 8:26-40). None, however, surpassed the Apostle Paul, a converted rabbi, in establishing an argument for Christianity by searching the scriptures "to see whether these things were so" (Acts 17:11). He worked careful arguments based on scripture into every letter. As the churches drew more and more converts from among the Gentiles, they held steadfastly to the importance of studying scriptures. "All scripture is inspired by God," the Apostle explained to Timothy, "and is useful for teaching, for reproof, for correction, and for training in righteousness, so that everyone who belongs to God may be proficient, equipped for every good work" (2 Tim. 3:16-17).

Many have asked why it is necessary to use the intellect in biblical interpretation. "If scriptures are the Word of God, of what use is critical scholarship? Why don't we just rely on the Spirit?"

First of all, we study scriptures because, as one early Christian discovered about Paul's writings, "some things in them [are] hard to understand" (2 Pet. 3:16). Like other complex and profound writings, the scriptures will scarcely reveal their insights to us unless we learn all we can about the author, purpose, date, place, circumstances of writing, and many other things. Different kinds of literature will pose different challenges. To wrestle the deep truths that we seek from these writings requires disciplined study using the best methods and information available.

More important, we put forth this effort because we want to have in ourselves the mind of Christ (Phil. 2:5), a love-guided, servant-oriented, humble mind. How do we develop such a mind? We do not just sit back and wait for the Spirit to bring about this change in us. Although God alone can effect such transformation in us, we know that we have to open ourselves to God and learn of God's will for us. Study involves us in the same eager searching of scriptures in which the saints have engaged through the centuries. As the popular author Richard Foster has said, "The Discipline of study is the primary vehicle to bring us to '*think* about [whatever is pure, whatever is lovely, whatever is gracious, if there is anything worthy of praise'" (Phil. 4:8).][2]

A group of devout Roman women set an example for us during the late fourth century. They gathered in the palace of Marcella on the Aventine Hill in Rome to study scriptures. Most of them were probably fluent in Greek, but they also learned Hebrew. When they learned that Jerome, the most noted biblical scholar of the day, had come to Rome in 382, Marcella persuaded him to lead them in their study. He did so reluctantly at first, but soon learned that Marcella and some of the others challenged even him in his thought and understanding. She plied him with questions and shared her interpretations. When he had to flee Rome and go to the Holy Land in 385, some of the Aventine Circle went with him. There they continued their eager search of the scriptures. Jerome dedicated much of his work in preparing the Vulgate Bible to one of them named Paula.

Tools for the Study of Scripture

In our study of scriptures we have to concern ourselves with two contexts—the original author's and our own. To interpret properly, we want to avoid reading our ideas and impressions into the document we are studying. Meaningful interpretation of the scriptures depends to a great extent upon proper understanding of each writing in the original language, culture, and context.

Language. An abundance of excellent English translations and paraphrases is available to serious students. A good translation is not literal. Rather, a careful translator will take the thoughts used by the original authors in their cultural setting and put them in modern terms that express the same ideas in our own cultural setting. Reading several versions of the same passage often helps us grasp its meaning.

As we choose various translations of scripture, we ought to exercise special care. Older translations can be misleading because even modern languages become dated. Words change. Take, for instance,

[In the community formed by Benedict], time was given for study and a more systematic approach to holy scripture and other writings but not as a prerequisite to letting God speak through a text or verse of the Bible. Accurate, academic dissection of the material was not the primary aim of being with the word. Instead the approach was to sit quietly in the presence of God and with open heart and mind to wait until the text touched a deep place within and invited the listener into conversation with its Author.

—Elizabeth J. Canham

the King James Version of 1 Thessalonians 4:15: "That we which are alive and remain unto the coming of the Lord shall not prevent [that is, precede or go before] them which are asleep." While perfectly intelligible in the seventeenth century, this translation will cause no small amount of confusion today because of the evolution of English. More important, the texts on which translations are based have improved with the discovery of new manuscripts and changes in technology. Also, the skill and knowledge of the translators will play an integral role in the quality and readability of the translations.

Culture. Language is only one part of culture with which interpreters need to deal in order to understand the scriptures and let them speak to the modern condition. Others include the psychology, physics, political perspective, and worldview of an author. Hebrew psychology, for example, contrasted quite noticeably with the Greek. Where the Greeks thought in terms of human beings in three parts— body, soul, and spirit—the Hebrews emphasized unity. Hebrew physics did not separate matter and spirit.

Context. Most of the books of the Bible were written in a simple enough style that we can understand the text as it stands, but they are clearer when we know their context. Context has to do with date, place, circumstances of writing, and other factors that help us interpret. The more you understand the context of a particular writing, for instance, that a certain text is actually a letter, the more likely you are to interpret accurately what the author was saying.

As an example from the Hebrew Scriptures, most scholars think that the eighth-century prophet Isaiah (742–701 B.C.E.) wrote only chapters 1–39 of Isaiah. Chapters 40–66 belong to the time of Cyrus of Persia (539 B.C.E.) and after. Proper interpretation of the message of Isaiah is helped by distinguishing these different contexts.

Determining the context of the Gospels and other New Testament writings poses a major challenge, but one that helps us glean their insights for us. It takes only a casual reading to see that John differs markedly from Matthew, Mark, and Luke—what are usually called the synoptic Gospels. John obviously wrote out of another context. Careful study of Matthew, Mark, and Luke shows that each of them fashioned his account of the good news in a different time and place, for a different audience.

The Limits of Study

The challenges of interpretation should not make us timid about reading scripture. A good study Bible will supply most of the basic information. The critical study of the scriptures, moreover, is not the most significant concern of spiritual formation. Historical and linguistic knowledge of scripture has its limits. Study helps us to use our minds to focus on God; but more important, it provides a framework for meditation, which is a kind of listening with the heart. Study is what Thomas Merton has called the "front porch" of meditation. "By study we seek the truth in books or in some other source outside our own minds. In meditation we strive to absorb what we have already taken in," he says.[3] The metaphor is helpful, for it reminds us that we must do more than learn about the Word of God. We want, rather, to know the God of the Word. Meditation, Merton adds, "seeks to possess the truth not only by knowledge but also by love."[4] In meditation, we seek to enter into God's presence, to listen to God's voice, and to respond in faithful and loving action. It is not accidental that monks were the copiers and illuminators of manuscripts, translators, and interpreters of scripture throughout much of Christian history. They had a desire for God that fostered a love of learning.[5] That love of learning focused, above all, on scriptures, and it was a learning both for mind and heart.

The reading of scripture is a spiritual discipline. One of the problems we have, however, is that when our reading of scripture becomes dry and doesn't seem to "do" anything for us any more, we tend to look somewhere else. . . . There is also the need to be willing to wait upon the Word, the necessity of offering up our reading of the scripture to God to be used as God chooses and when God chooses.

—M. Robert Mulholland Jr.

DAILY EXERCISES

The core of studying scripture is mental attention and careful listening. We listen with a desire to hear God's voice and do God's will. In this way, reflection on scripture becomes a means by which God leads us in becoming the persons we are called to be. This week prepare yourself with prayer, asking to be open to God. On first reading, ask yourself questions such as, "What do I need to know in order to hear this passage in its context? What general truths does this passage convey about God, me, and my relationships?" If you have a good study Bible, look at the notes on each passage. On second reading, ask yourself questions such as, "What aspect of this passage invites me to deeper exploration? What does God want me to hear or call me to do?"

EXERCISE 1

Read Genesis 3:1-13. This story speaks to the challenge of paying attention to God. On first reading, you might consider what the story reveals about the qualities of relationship that God desires, or blocks that we experience in listening to God. On second reading, you might pause at points along the way to allow words and images to search you. For example, with verse 8, how has God been "walking" in the garden of my life lately? With verse 9, how do I respond to God's searching call, "Where are you?" With verse 13, what gets stirred up in me when God asks, "What is this that you have done?" Record your thoughts and feelings.

EXERCISE 2

Read Genesis 32:22-32. This story is about Jacob's going to the river where he wrestles with God and is changed. On first reading, you might explore the larger context: What was Jacob worried about, and why did he go to the river alone? (This larger context can be seen in chapter 27 and chapter 32:3-21.) Or what does the story suggest about solitude and what one must do to gain time alone with God? On second reading, you might get in touch with parts of you that identify with Jacob's situation or your need to be away from others for a while. What must you do to gain that time alone with God? What will you and God wrestle about? How do you respond to God's question, "What is your name?" How might God express the promise of your life: "You shall no longer be called _____, but _____"?

EXERCISE 3

Read Psalm 81. This summons to worship turns into an expression of God's deep disappointment over our spiritual deafness. God appeals to us to listen and enjoy the benefit of divine guidance. On first reading, you might consider what this psalm reveals about the heart of God and about the hearts of the Hebrew people. On second reading, you might pause to listen to the "voice I had not known" regarding the condition of your own heart. What is the character of your heart when it is stubborn, and what have been some of the consequences? What is the character of your heart when it is listening, and what difference would a listening heart make in your life?

EXERCISE 4

Read Mark 10:17-22. This story is about a rich man who wanted to do what was required—within limits—to inherit eternal life. On first reading, you might note the contrast between the man's favorable words to Jesus and his reluctance to obey, or reflect on what limited this man's response to Jesus' call. On second reading, you might explore what keeps you from fully living your profession of faith in the "Good Teacher." Listen for what Jesus is saying about the one thing you lack. As you do so, see Jesus looking at you with love, nonetheless.

EXERCISE 5

Read John 10:1-10. This passage is about Jesus as the Good Shepherd. On first reading, note the differences Jesus describes between the shepherd and the thief. On the second reading, explore your own

awareness of the Good Shepherd's voice. What are its qualities? What other voices imitate God, appeal for your attention, and take over your life? How do you tell the difference between them and the voice of God in you?

Review your journal entries for the week in preparation for the group meeting.

Meditating on the Word

There are many kinds of Christian meditation, but above all it is listening to God through the scriptures, ruminating on the Word, a deep conversation of hearing and responding. In meditation we read not just for information; we probe, ponder, and explore so that the words of scripture become for us the Word of God in our lives.

The Practice of Meditation

The Hebrew tradition that centered on the Law encouraged meditation. In Deuteronomy, the "book of the Law," Moses instructed the people to "keep these words that I am commanding you today in your heart" (Deut. 6:6). He also commanded Joshua to "meditate on [the Law] day and night, so that you may be careful to act in accordance with all that is written in it" (Josh. 1:8).

The Book of Psalms opens, "Happy are those . . . [whose] delight is in the law of the Lord, and on his law they meditate day and night" (Ps. 1:1-2). Another psalmist entreated, "Let the words of my mouth and the meditation of my heart be acceptable to you, O Lord, my rock and my redeemer" (Ps. 19:14; see also 49:3). Another asked, "How can young people keep [God's statutes] pure?" and answered, "By guarding [them] according to your word. . . . I treasure your word in my heart, so that I may not sin against you" (Ps. 119:9, 11).

The gospel is not a doctrine of the tongue, but of life. It cannot be grasped by reason and memory only, but it is fully understood when it possesses the whole soul, and penetrates to the inner recesses of the heart.

—John Calvin

In the second century B.C.E. the Jewish scribe Jesus ben Sirach spoke about the searching attention scriptures must receive well beyond what we would call study. "Happy is he who gives his mind to wisdom and meditates on understanding; happy is he who reflects on her ways and ponders her secrets" (Ecclus. 14:20-21, REB). Meditation on the Law means "not only thinking about the Law, studying the Law, but living it with a full, or relatively full, understanding of God's purpose in manifesting to us [God's] will."[1]

Jesus of Nazareth doubtless spent many hours meditating on the Hebrew Scriptures, just as the rabbis did. His use of scripture in engaging his critics would seem to make this clear. And the rabbi Saul (turned apostle Paul) urged his converts to meditate: "Finally, beloved, whatever is true, whatever is honorable, whatever is just, whatever is pure, whatever is pleasing, whatever is commendable, if there is any excellence and if there is anything worthy of praise, think about these things" (Phil. 4:8; see also Col. 3:2). He uses the word *think* in the sense of reflection or pondering.

Christian meditation blossomed uniquely in the deserts of Egypt and Arabia among the hermits and monks of the fourth through the sixth centuries who sought purity of heart in order that they might see God. In these early centuries of the church, few of the desert fathers and mothers would have owned complete Bibles or been able to read them, but the Sayings of the desert monks speak often of the benefits of meditating on scripture. Both individually and communally, the monks said the words of a particular text orally, mulled them over in the mind, chewed on them, and slowly digested them. Such practices helped them abandon themselves to God for the strengthening and transforming of their lives.[2]

The meditative wisdom of the desert fathers and mothers stood behind the Benedictine spiritual tradition. In the sixth century, Benedict of Nursia founded one of the notable monastic orders. The Rule of Benedict divided the monks' day into three parts: six hours of manual labor, four hours of the daily office (chanting the psalms), and four hours in spiritual reading and prayer. The time of reading might include other devotional writings such as the lives of saints, but it

focused, above all, on the scriptures. The objective was "a more intimate communion with God not only in the future *but also here and now*."[3] Such communion requires not just knowledge but also love.

Approaches to Meditation

What does meditation involve? Your approach will depend to some extent on your personality. Some persons want to listen slowly to the words of scripture. They may prefer to break the text down into its component parts, pausing to reflect on each thought that comes to mind. Some passages lend themselves to such an approach. The Beatitudes, for instance, halt you in your tracks with their reversal of logic and make you think. "Blessed are the meek, for they will inherit the earth" (Matt. 5:5). You might ask, "Hmm? How could that be? What we usually see is the triumph of the powerful, not the meek. How could the meek inherit the earth? Did Jesus inherit the earth? What did Francis of Assisi or Gandhi or Martin Luther King or Mother Teresa accomplish by gentleness? Don't people gain more by aggressiveness?"

That is one level of meditative reading: asking what the scripture could have meant to the people of Jesus' day and could mean to us in general. There is, however, another level: to ask, "What is it saying to me? Does the text have a 'word' for me in this day and time? All too often I am anything but meek or gentle—in driving, in pressing my argument, in replying to someone whose words have hurt me. And where has that led me? How has this affected my relationships? The meek seem to get run over. But what is the consequence of the power games we play? Constant conflict? Violence completely out of control? Am I willing to hear Jesus' revolutionary challenge to a lifestyle of meekness? 'Lord, gentle me. Help me to understand what it means to be meek.'"

Some persons' way of meditating with scripture may rely more on intuition, "apprehending it in its wholeness as beauty rather than as truth."[4] Take Psalm 139, that wonderful psalm about God's inescapable nearness. The author seemingly wants to escape God,

> *The meditation of Scripture centers on internalizing and personalizing the passage. The written Word becomes a living word addressed to you.*
> —Richard J. Foster

but then finds God in the midst of all creation. In the first seven verses the writer speaks of God's intimate knowledge of us. God knows us better than we know ourselves.

The psalmist goes on to reflect on the fact that there is no place to flee from God's presence. Verse 8 states the disturbing yet comforting truth: "If I ascend to heaven, you are there; if I make my bed in Sheol, you are there." Two words jump out at me in my meditation on the last half of the verse—*make* and *Sheol*. The psalmist doesn't say, "If I trip and fall in." He says, "If I make." That says to me, "Glenn, you cannot mess your life up to the extent that God will abandon you." In Hebrew thought, Sheol is by definition where God is not. For our psalmist, God is to be found everywhere. "If I take the wings of the morning and settle at the farthest limits of the sea, even there your hand shall lead me, and your right hand shall hold me fast" (139:9-10).

In the next chapter, we will explore how the use of imagination can help us in our meditation on scripture. The more vividly we can enter into the scripture in imagination, the better. If we are meditating on a story in which there are animals, says Ignatius, smell the manure! Meditation allows for diverse approaches that will help us be attentive to God.

A Basic Pattern of Meditation

> *Lectio is undertaken in the conviction that God's word is meant to be a "good" word; that is, something carrying God's own life in a way that benefits the one who receives it faithfully.*
>
> —Norvene Vest

Benedict of Nursia urged his communities to practice a regular rhythm of spiritual reading of scripture. Over the following centuries, the Benedictines gave the practice of meditation on scripture a more defined form. They outlined a simple but profound pattern that integrates reading, meditation, and prayer. This pattern or method has been widely used through the centuries both by Roman Catholics and Protestants. It is often referred to by its Latin title, *lectio divina* (which means "sacred reading or holy reading"). In *lectio divina*, the seeker is invited to choose a place and time conducive to reflection and prayer, where he or she can be comfortable and undisturbed. Typically, *lectio divina* is described in four phases or stages. These reflect different dynamics of our praying and reading and could be more accurately described as movements of the mind and heart.

The first stage is a slow reading of the scripture passage. Usually one selects a short passage since the focus is not on the amount of text to be covered but on the depth and concentration of the reading. Frequently it helps to read the passage more than once. Images and words can easily go unnoticed in only one reading. We must be willing to stay with portions of the text that seem to be speaking to us and allow for times of silence and rereading as they seem helpful.

The second stage focuses on meditation. We begin to reflect intently on the scripture passage. This is the heart of meditation where we seek to hear and explore the special words, images, or phrases through which God may be speaking. We allow the words to sink into our consciousness and help us look at ourselves and our relationship with God.

A contemporary author, Elizabeth Canham, has written of this experience during a meditation on Mark 1:35-39. In this text, Jesus has gotten up early to pray, but Simon and the others find him and tell him that they have been hunting for him. In fact, they report, "Everyone is searching for you." Jesus answers that he is ready to go to the neighboring towns and continue to proclaim the message for which he has come. And so he goes to continue his ministry of preaching and healing. In Elizabeth's meditation, this passage immediately reminds her of how much pressure she experiences in her own life and helps her see how the demands on her time have generated resentment in her. She begins to think of Jesus, how he set his priorities with his early rising for prayer and yet, in response to the words of the disciples, how readily he took up again his ministry to a hurting world. She finds herself longing to be present to God in prayer so that she can sense more clearly her call to service. She wants to receive new energy and vision to go to those places of service and to overcome the resentment that colors her perspective. Her meditation has enabled her to see what is happening in her life and also to see what God may be offering to her.[5]

The third stage of *lectio* is prayer. After meditation we move naturally into a time of prayer, expressing our response to what we have heard. We speak directly to God of our needs and struggles, our repentance and our gratitude. We open ourselves to the new life God is offering and ask for the grace to do what we are being called to do. The scripture passage has moved from an external reading to a word that dwells within us.

In the last stage, we come to an experience of contemplation, a time of quietness and resting. Our words cease, and we simply abide in God's presence. We trust ourselves to the One who loves us. It is a time of letting go and being receptive to what God seeks to give us at that moment.

Of course, these stages or phases do not always progress in such an orderly, sequential way. We may move easily among the various stages—sometimes "caught" by a word and immediately wanting to pray or desiring to pause and rest in an awareness of God's enfolding love. Sometimes our prayer may take the form of writing. Whatever the movement, we are expressing our desire that God will give us a word of life and that we will be able to hear and respond.

Helpful Guidelines

Thomas Merton has given some guidelines to help us in meditation. One important consideration is "the proper atmosphere of prayer," which basically means you need a quiet place away from normal distractions—a room in your home, a chapel, a garden, a park. You can meditate with others or by yourself. "The most important thing," Merton says, "is to seek silence, tranquillity, recollection and peace."[6]

Some of us may have to give ourselves permission to meditate. We belong to a society that values activity and views time spent in solitude as laziness. If you hold this view, argue a case for yourself. Say, "I need this for my re-creation. Others can't stand to live with me if I don't do this! I will become more collected and get more done in the long run if I do this. I may 'burn out' if I don't. After all, I am not doing nothing!"

As for the meditation itself, the crucial point is sincerity. You will get something out of scripture even when the exercise becomes routine, but the routine will be a far cry from what you want. The desert monks and the Puritans spoke often about "compunction." Compunction has to do with a recognition that we are in need of God. Like Paul, we confess, "We do not know how to pray as we ought" (Rom. 8:26), and we call on the Spirit to help us in our weakness.

As we wrestle sincerely with the words of scripture, they begin to speak to our condition. Abba Isaac, one of the desert saints, explained how he and others related the psalms to their life situations: "When we use the words, we remember, by a kind of meditative association, our own circumstances and struggles, the results of our negligence or earnestness, the mercies of God's providence or the temptations of the devil, the subtle and slippery sins of forgetfulness or human frailty or unthinking ignorance."[7]

Meditation requires concentration. Teresa of Avila, the sixteenth-century Carmelite reformer and mystic, offered a homely image of meditation for beginners. For those unaccustomed to the practice, she warned that meditation may tire the mind, for it is like lifting water out of a cistern with a bucket. Sometimes we may find the cistern dry, and always we will have distractions.[8] Indeed, we may experience our minds flitting around "like a hummingbird on holiday."[9] The advice of Teresa, who struggled for twenty years to learn how to pray, was that you not give up. Just wait for the Spirit to lift you.[10] If distractions come, be aware of them and then let them go in order to resume your listening.

Dietrich Bonhoeffer, the German theologian who opposed Nazi ideology, sounded like a Benedictine monk when he required the seminarians at Finkenwalde to meditate thirty minutes every morning for a week on the same passage of scripture. In *Life Together* he explained what should take place:

> In our meditation we ponder the chosen text on the strength of the promise that it has something utterly personal to say to us for this day and for our Christian life, that it is not only God's Word for the Church, but also God's Word for us individually. We expose ourselves to the

It might also be of use, if, while we read [the Bible], we were frequently to pause, and examine ourselves by what we read, both with regard to our hearts and lives. . . . And whatever light you then receive, should be used to the uttermost, and that immediately. Let there be no delay. . . . So shall you find this word to be indeed the power of God unto present and eternal salvation.

—John Wesley

specific word until it addresses us personally. And when we do this, we are doing no more than the simplest, untutored Christian does every day; we read God's Word as God's Word for us.[11]

We should not expect to get through the entire passage in one sitting. One sentence or even one word may arrest us. We need not express our thought or prayer in words or discover new ideas or have unexpected, extraordinary experiences. What matters is that the Word "penetrates and dwells within us."[12] We want to ponder these things in our hearts, as Mary pondered what the angels told the shepherds (Luke 2:19). Bonhoeffer's encouraging word is this: "We must center our attention on the Word alone and leave consequences to its action."[13]

DAILY EXERCISES

This week you will begin to practice a pattern for reading scripture prayerfully (or praying with scripture) called *lectio divina* (pronounced LEX-ee-oh dih-VEE-nuh), which is Latin for "divine or sacred reading." Classic descriptions of *lectio divina* list a sequence of four movements: *lectio* (reading), *meditatio* (ruminating and reflecting), *oratio* (responding to God), and *contemplatio* (receiving and resting in God).

Lectio—Slowly read a brief passage of scripture. Read it as though you are hearing it read to you. Read it silently and aloud. Experiment by reading it with different emphases and inflections.

Meditatio—Mull over the text; internalize the words. Listen for the phrases that stand out for you as you read the passage. Turn them over in your mind. Reflect on why these words catch your attention, what they bring to mind, and what they mean for you today. Jot down in your journal the meaningful words, noting associations, reactions, feelings, or challenges.

Oratio—Turn your meditation from dialogue with yourself to dialogue with God, which is prayer. Share with God in all honesty your reflections, questions, or feelings. Offer your thanksgiving, confession, petitions, or intercessions as they arise within during your dialogue with God. Listen for God's response and inner nudging.

Contemplatio—Rest your mental activity and trust yourself completely to God's love and care. Relax in God's presence. Pick a phrase from the text to which you can return again and again as you keep your attention on God. Allow this prayer-phrase to sustain your presence to God throughout the day. After a few minutes of "practicing the presence of God" in this way, you might close with the Lord's Prayer, a song, or a final moment of grateful silence.

Capture your meditation, prayer, and the new insights and possibilities God gave you through your journal. Consider one token—one small act—you can offer today in grateful response to God's life-giving word to you during this special time with the scripture.

Classical writers have compared this process to eating. In reading, you bite off a small chunk of text. Through meditation, you chew on it, extracting the nutrients and juices. In prayer, you swallow, incorporating the results of your meditation and allowing them to nourish your life. And in contemplation, you savor the good taste left in your mouth, celebrate the gift of God's word to you, and embrace the new life you have received. *Lectio divina* is more than a method; it is a way of life rooted in daily listening to the Word of God.

As you move through the daily exercises this week, you will be using the four movements of *lectio divina*. Before you begin, prepare yourself for a period of time to be with God. Quiet yourself by breathing slowly and deeply. Prepare to be personally addressed by a word from God. Pray before you begin your *lectio* each day, "May these words become to me the Word of God." Enter into each passage with the question, "What is God saying to me through this text?" Honor the natural movements of the words from the eyes and lips (in reading) to the mind (in reflection) to the heart (in prayerful responses to God) to the spirit of your life (in receiving God's gift and resting in God's love). Let the Spirit guide you in your journey to God through each text. Consider the written suggestions below as just that—suggestions if you need help getting started.

EXERCISE 1

Read Psalm 23 silently and then aloud as though for the first time.

Meditate slowly on each verse. Linger with images that are rich in meaning. Explore why these images attract you.

Pray to God with your thoughts and feelings (gratitude, joy, or longing). Tell God where you need what the words of the psalm convey. Open your heart in all honesty, then listen.

Contemplate the gift of God's care. Trust your life to God in situations that concern you.

Record your experience.

EXERCISE 2

Read Psalm 27 through once, then again—one line at a time slowly.

Reflect on meanings for you in each phrase; for example, "The Lord," "is my light," "and my salvation."

Respond to the question, "Of whom shall I be afraid?" Tell the Lord the fears that control you. Personalize each verse as a way to talk with God; then listen.

Rest in God's light with an affirmation such as verse 14: "Wait for the Lord; be strong, and let your heart take courage."

Record your experience.

EXERCISE 3

Read Matthew 16:13-16 and any study notes that your Bible may provide.

Reflect on Jesus' questions as though they were addressed to you. Who do people today say Jesus is? Who do you say Jesus is? Explore your affirmations and questions.

Respond to Jesus directly. Dialogue with him in prayer, and listen for his responses and promptings.

Rest in Jesus' remarkable trust in us to be his church. Resolve to act as you are led.

Record your insights.

EXERCISE 4

Read Luke 12:22-32 several times, and repeat the verses that draw you in more deeply.

Meditate on verse 25. Name your worries, needs, or preoccupations about the future.

Converse with Jesus about any of your reservations concerning his counsel "not to worry" and "strive only for the kingdom." Listen for his response.

Soak in the assurance of how much God values you and of how free you are to let go of those things that cause you worry.

Record your insights and thoughts.

EXERCISE 5

Read Romans 8:31-39. Return to a verse that best captures for you the meaning of the passage.

Reflect on what it means to live with such faith in God's love and care.

Respond in prayer by telling God of circumstances where you or other people do in fact feel separated from an awareness of God's love. Pay attention to the leading of the Spirit.

Rest in God's presence as you offer each circumstance to God, asking for faith to say in each, "For I am convinced that neither death, nor life, . . . nor anything else in all creation, will be able to separate us from the love of God in Christ Jesus our Lord" (vv. 38-39).

Record your insights.

Review your journal entries for the week in preparation for the group meeting.

Part 2, Week 4
Directing Imagination

As the preceding lesson mentioned, meditation on scripture can also benefit from the use of imagination, entering into scriptures in the way a child listens to a good storyteller. You have witnessed that, haven't you? Children will get up and act out part of the story. They will answer questions that haven't been asked. They make the story their story.

The more vivid your imagination, the more deeply the story will fix itself in your memory and thought and the more deeply it will penetrate into the unconscious, to use the terminology of Jungian analysts. What takes place resembles what happens when you dream, except that you are awake. You are dealing with scripture both at the conscious level—seeing, hearing, touching, tasting, smelling, and reflecting—and at the subconscious level. As a result, meditation can leave its mark on both levels.

In the Jungian understanding, our human psyche is much larger and more complex than the part that operates on the conscious and rational levels. The unconscious level accounts in many ways for who we are and how we act as persons. We experience all kinds of things from outside ourselves at the unconscious level. Life experiences, some good and some bad, burrow their way into the unconscious and remain hidden until another event causes them to spring into consciousness again.

Imagination is the capacity to make connections between the visible and the invisible, between heaven and earth, between present and past, between present and future. For Christians, whose largest investment is in the invisible, the imagination is indispensable, for it is only by means of the imagination that we can see reality whole, in context.

—Eugene H. Peterson

Imagination, like dreams, comes into play not only in our observing and thinking processes but also in the vastly larger unconscious. Human imagination is highly complex. Like dreaming, it deals in symbols that often have far greater effect than words or thoughts. They touch us subtly at the deepest levels of our being. Take, for example, Paul's experience recorded in 2 Corinthians 12:1-10. Fourteen years earlier, he said he had experienced being caught up into heaven or paradise. Whether that happened in or out of the body, he couldn't say. There he saw and heard things that no mortal can repeat—visions and revelations of the Lord. Repeatable or not, they affected him profoundly. They transformed his life forever. Visionary experiences like Paul's are generally conveyed through symbols and images.

Entering Scripture with Imagination

How does imagination with scripture work? First, it works best with narrative portions of the Bible: stories with characters, dialogue, and movement. Passages from the Gospels or Acts are ideal for this kind of meditation. By using the imagination, we carry on a conversation with biblical figures and events through which God chose to speak. We try to become a part of the story, picturing it and identifying with the persons described. As we enter into the story this way, it can open up insight, inspire us, and enliven us.

Two remarkable Christian leaders viewed the proper direction of imagination in biblical meditation as a key to the holy life. One was Ignatius of Loyola (1491–1556), the great Catholic reformer and founder of the Society of Jesus (Jesuits). The other was Richard Baxter (1615–91), a very influential Puritan English pastor and writer. These two differed in the way they expressed the goal of imaginative meditation. For Ignatius, the goal was to prepare the soul "to free itself of all inordinate attachments" and to seek and discover God's will for one's life.[1] For Baxter, it was to attain "the saints' everlasting rest."[2] Today perhaps we would express the goal in terms of intimacy with God.

Surprisingly, Ignatius and Baxter agreed as to the method of meditation—entering into scriptures imaginatively and allowing them

Frequency in heavenly contemplation is particularly important, to prevent a shyness between God and thy soul. Frequent society breeds familiarity, and familiarity increases love and delight, and makes us bold in our addresses. The chief end of this duty is, to have acquaintance and fellowship with God; and therefore, if thou come but seldom to it, thou wilt keep thyself a stranger still.
—Richard Baxter

to touch and shape one's life. Scriptural meditation assumes an intimate and deep familiarity with the Bible, not just casual acquaintance. Devout Puritans, convinced that they would find answers to life's most urgent questions only in the scriptures, spent hours in study and meditation, poring over the Bible and memorizing all they could. John Bunyan, the seventeenth-century author of *The Pilgrim's Progress*, said that, during his traumatic battle with manic depression, he "was never out of the Bible, either by reading or meditation."[3] Puritans expected familiar scripture texts to dart into their minds and hearts and give them needed guidance.

To prepare for this meditation, Baxter gave similar advice to that of Thomas Merton. Find a place where you can become quiet and consider carefully the disposition of your heart. The heart must be freed from as many distractions as possible. Then, set about this work "with the greatest solemnity of heart and mind."[4] The key to directing the heart toward "heavenly rest" or intimacy with God lies in exercising the affections: love, desire, hope, courage, and joy. Since emotions can be tricky and misleading, however, we must take care that they move us closer to God. That is the task of "consideration."[5]

For Baxter, consideration as a form of meditation relied on imagination and could draw from the deep well of memorized scriptures. He painted word pictures in which he contrasted scenes of heaven with scenes on earth to help the devout aspire to heaven. Like Ignatius, he wanted vivid imagination of the glories of heaven and the trials of earth. In order to inspire Christians to consider the glories of heaven with deep feeling, Baxter encouraged sensory imagination in much the same way as Ignatius. Listen to Baxter's own words as he encourages a meditation on the vision of heavenly glory from the Book of Revelation. It is adapted here into modern English so we may understand it more clearly (remember that to "suppose" is essentially to imagine):

> Draw as strong suppositions as you can from your senses for the helping of your affections. . . . Suppose yourself now beholding the city of God; and that you have been companion with John in his survey of its glory; and have seen the thrones, the Majesty, the heavenly hosts, the

[In meditation,] get thy heart as clear from the world as thou canst. Wholly lay by the thoughts of thy business, troubles, enjoyments, and every thing that may take up any room in thy soul. Get it as empty as thou possibly canst, that it may be the more capable of being filled with God.

—Richard Baxter

shining splendor which he saw: suppose . . . that you have seen the saints clothed in white robes, with palms of victory in their hands: suppose you have heard the song of Moses and of the Lamb; or do even now hear them praising and glorifying the living God. . . . Get the liveliest picture of them in your mind which you possibly can. Meditate on them, as if you were all the while beholding them, and as if you were even hearing the hallelujahs while you are thinking of them, till you can say, "I think I see a glimpse of the glory! I think I hear the shouts of joy and praise! I think I stand by Abraham and David, Peter and Paul . . . I think I even see the Son of God appearing in the clouds. . . . I think I hear him say, Come, you blessed of my Father!"[6]

We can see how Baxter encourages his readers to place themselves imaginatively into certain settings described in the Bible. Later, while illustrating this method with one of his own meditations, Baxter breaks into a spontaneous dialogue between Christ and his own soul, a device Ignatius also frequently commended for taking personally to heart the message of scripture.

Baxter cautiously suggested that the devout might assist their meditation with the use of sensory objects if they were careful not to actually draw the objects, as Roman Catholics did. In our day most Protestants are less hesitant to use paintings, icons, stained glass windows, statues, and other symbols for meditation. In an age of visual learning many are rediscovering how traditional Christian icons may draw us "into closer communion with the God of love."[7]

Example of Meditation

Here is an example of one of my own meditations on Jesus' encounter with Zacchaeus in Luke 19:1-10. In my mind's eye I imagine myself as Zacchaeus that day as Jesus passed through Jericho on his way to Jerusalem. I am a "head tax collector," not a nice position to be in. Tax collectors are not highly regarded in our own society today, even though they work for us, "the government of the people." I can just imagine what those people clamoring around Jesus think about me, a Jew, when I collect taxes for the Romans who occupy our country. To make matters worse, I have been known to skim money off in order to get rich.

Also, I am small. I am so short that I have to run and scramble up a big sycamore tree just to see Jesus. Little people often have to be inventive to survive. I get there just as Jesus starts to pass by.

But to my amazement, he doesn't go on past. He stops, looks up, and says, "Zacchaeus, hurry and get down from there, for I've got to stay at your house today." Oh, wow! I almost fall out of that tree. I expect him to look every which way but up, to look right on past me lest people think he associates with the likes of me, or to give me that withering look so many others do. But he doesn't. He looks me right in the eye and invites himself to my house.

What do I feel? What else but inexpressible joy? Joy! Joy! Jesus has given the precious gift of attention and acceptance. Not only does he look me in the eye; he asks me to serve as his host. But does he realize what he is doing?

Now I pause for a little "meditative association." I begin to think about times when I have experienced the hurt of inattention the way Zacchaeus did. One time I went to a party and struck up a conversation with someone, and she kept sweeping the room with her eyes looking for someone more interesting to talk to. Another time I tried to present a new proposal to my colleagues and found that they did not share my excitement. They listened politely but showed little response to my ideas. Then I also thought of the times that I had experienced the pain of rejection.

But here, at last, is one whose love is wide enough to embrace even a tax collector. Whom will he not accept? If I doubt his acceptance, I need only look at what happens next.

See the price Jesus pays immediately. He no sooner gets to my house than the muttering starts, the pretended cries of disbelief: "He has gone in to have lunch with a sinful man."

I might start to worry again. But by now I have had a change of heart and I say, "See, sir, I will give half of everything I own to the poor. And if I have defrauded anyone, I will repay fourfold." I imagine the thoughts and feelings that have led to this change of heart in me.

Now I observe Jesus' response. Once again, he does not disappoint. Not only has Jesus accepted me, a universally despised person;

The scriptures are a vast repository of human dramas, and offer us endless scripts for exploring our feelings, understandings, and commitments. Only a little imagination makes them come alive with power and efficacy for contemporary living.

—John Killinger

I learned to listen while I read. Sometimes I would hear nothing except the words of my reading. More often, I was simply conscious that the passages were entering mind and heart and becoming part of me. But increasingly there were times when some aspect of what I was reading came home to me with such sudden strength and clarity that I was left with no doubt that God had something to say not just to the psalmist, the prophet, or the disciple— but to me.

—Avery Brooke

he even affirms me. No, not because of my promises, but because of his love. "Today salvation has come to this house, because he too is a son of Abraham. For the Son of Man came to seek out and to save the lost." Oh, good thing Jesus was inside the house when he said that. These people who adored him just a little while before would have murdered him! The very idea, calling me, a despicable tax collector, "a son of Abraham."

Your meditation on this passage might lead you to different feelings and images, based on your lived experience in relation to the scripture text. The meditation has led me to hear again the affirmation in this story, the same affirmation we get from the cross. As one hymn puts it, "There's a wideness in God's mercy like the wideness of the sea." And as Paul reminds us in Romans 8, nothing in all the world can separate us from the love of God. Ponder that assurance a while. I invite you to transfer it from your head to your heart. That is the goal of meditation.

DAILY EXERCISES

Before you begin the exercises for the week, remember to read the new chapter and write your notes, responses, questions, and concerns in your journal. This week's passages move through Luke's version of the Christmas story and help us to use our imaginations in meditating on scripture. Please try to follow the instructions even if you find them difficult or uncomfortable. Remember to write in your journal as you ponder the questions and/or after you have finished your contemplation.

EXERCISE 1

Read Luke 1:5-23. Go back through Zechariah's story and put yourself in the place of the man who was "getting on in years." Visualize what you are doing in the sanctuary, then what you see and feel when the angel first appears. How do your feelings change when the angel tells you that "your wife Elizabeth will bear you a son"? Imagine an honest conversation with the angel about the news. Capture the dialogue in writing, if possible. Imagine holding the news in silence for several months. Note what your imaginings with this story churn up in you—about unrevealed promise in your life, long-held prayers, or your ability to change. Pray to the Lord, and rest in God's promise.

EXERCISE 2

Read Luke 1:24-25. Try to put yourself in the story in the place of Elizabeth, a woman beyond childbearing years. Imagine how you learn of Zechariah's experience and discover what has happened. What is your reaction? Why do you decide to go into seclusion, and how does it help you? Imagine how you spend your time and what you are pondering and praying about during those five months apart. Reflect on the ways you identify with Elizabeth. For example, is God trying to tell you about something new happening in your life? Would some time apart help it become a reality?

EXERCISE 3

Read Luke 1:26-38. After reading the story of the Annunciation, go back through the story slowly in your imagination, putting yourself in Mary's place. Try to imagine yourself as Mary, hearing the angel's message. Where are you? What do you see and hear? What range of emotions do you feel? How do you respond to the angel? How does the "Holy Spirit . . . come upon you"? Reflect on what your imaginings with the story stir within you. What connections do you make with the divine promise in your life? Compare your response to Mary's response.

EXERCISE 4

Read Luke 2:8-20. Identify with the shepherds' story and their changes of emotion. What is the good news that you hear from the angel? Let your heart fill with song: carols, choruses, or portions of Handel's *Messiah*. Write your own words of praise. Trace your search for Mary and Joseph and the child. When you find them, what do you see, smell, or feel? What do you actually say to them? Reflect on what surprised you as you experienced the story in your imagination.

EXERCISE 5

Read Luke 2:22-38. Imagine yourself as a bystander in the crowd when Mary and Joseph bring Jesus to the Temple. Close your eyes and picture the scene as vividly as you can, using all five senses. Watch the story unfold as Simeon and Anna play their parts. Feel free to refer to the text, but hold the scene in your mind. If you would like to interact in some way—speak to Simeon, hold the baby and offer your own praise—go ahead. Afterward, write about any actions you took in the scene, your reactions, feelings, thoughts. Spend a few moments reflecting on what your meditation may mean for your life.

Remember to review your journal entries for the week in preparation for the group meeting.

Part 2, Week 5
Group Meditation with Scripture

lthough Protestants have held firmly to the conviction that every individual who seeks the Word of God may find it in the scriptures, they have had to recognize also the values of listening to God in the company of other believers. Corporate meditation can contribute in a number of ways to listening for the Word of God in scripture.

I can find my true identity, my true name, only by sharing in the life of the community, the people of God, and taking my proper place there.

—Mary Jean Manninen

The Benefits of Group Meditation

Group meditation on scripture broadens perspectives. Culture exerts a powerful influence over the way we listen and what we hear. It beats, hammers, molds, and engraves us to such an extent that we may hear what the culture says rather than what God says through scripture. The more restricted our cultural experience, the more limited our ability to hear God through the scriptures. A group may also exhibit a narrow perspective. The more diverse the group, the more likely it is that the members will be able to broaden one another's outlook. It is amazing how many and diverse are the perspectives that participants hear in a gathering of the World Council of Churches where more than three hundred denominations from 120 nations are represented. Although few of us have opportunities to share in such meetings, we can find groups that will expand our individual outlook.

Group meditation can correct individual idiosyncrasies. People who are serious about meditation on scripture have sometimes come up with far-fetched interpretations of scripture and have blamed God as well as the devil for all sorts of questionable thoughts. Taken out of context, individual passages of scripture often yield curious conclusions. When John Bunyan used the Puritan method of relying on scriptures to dart into his mind and heart and tell him whether he was one of the "elect," for instance, it put him on a roller coaster emotionally. Sometimes he heard a reassuring word, "Whoever comes to me I will in no wise cast out." Most of the time, however, he did not get a positive word. The passage about Esau selling his birthright kept springing up. He became convinced that he was a modern Esau who had sold not his natural but his Christian birthright. He feared that he had committed the unpardonable sin. His moods rocketed up and down. He could never come to an even keel. What helped most to rescue him was the pastor John Gifford and participation in a little group at Gifford's home.[1] In his classic allegory *The Pilgrim's Progress*, Bunyan's main character Christian identified this church at Bedford as Interpreter's House, where he had seen "things rare and profitable; things pleasant, dreadful, things to make me stable in what I have begun to take in hand."[2] Group interaction forces participants to think more deeply and carefully about what they hear and how they apply insights.

Sharing insights with others should increase our confidence that we are listening well and hearing correctly. It is possible that only one person may hear God rightly and that a whole crowd may be wrong. Otherwise, we would have no prophets. Think of Martin Luther, father of the Protestant Reformation, standing against the entire German Parliament declaring that he could not act against his conscience:

> Unless I am convicted by Scripture or by right reason (for I trust neither in popes nor in councils, since they have often erred and contradicted themselves)—unless I am thus convinced, I am bound by the texts of the Bible, my conscience is captive to the Word of God, I neither can nor will recant anything, since it is neither right nor safe to act against conscience.[3]

But each of us, no matter how learned or spiritually mature, must shudder when we find ourselves in such a position and admit that we might be wrong. Group members who take seriously their corporate listening will, more often than not, come nearer the truth than an isolated individual.

We should get some joy out of discovering an insight with others. What pleasure in knowing that we are not alone in the search! Another's insight may amplify, clarify, or add new perspective to our own. Someone else in the group may put into words the experience we have but cannot express.

Description of Group Meditation

How does group meditation with scripture work? There are undoubtedly various ways to do it, but most would need to include the following elements: (1) an opening period of silence or some other centering exercise, (2) a reading aloud of a particular passage of scripture, (3) a second period of silence to permit each person to meditate long enough to enter the passage with the most vivid imagination or serious reflection, (4) a time of sharing insights that came to each person, and (5) some sort of closure.[4]

Initiating group meditation with a time of silence permits participants to get away from the day's distractions, become attentive to God, and direct their minds to what God may communicate through the text. Most will arrive still jangling from the day's activities, driving through traffic, memories of unpleasant encounters or other distractions that get in the way of listening. A period of silence will let people refocus before they try to listen. If members have trouble getting settled, the group leader may want to use some kind of relaxation exercise or other centering process, such as a song or simple spoken prayer; but silence is often the best preparation for listening.

Christian meditation has focused especially on the Gospels because in them we have "the story of stories," the story of Jesus.[5] This would not preclude the use of other scriptures, of course, for they form part of God's self-disclosure to us. Many have received deep nourishment

When we limit truth to our way of seeing, we often fail to receive the many surprises God offers us each day. When we open our eyes, and seek to see— through the eyes of a child or from perspectives different from our own— we are often able to experience God's world (and God) in ways we never imagined.

—Dwight W. Vogel
and Linda J. Vogel

meditating on the psalms. If a group continues week by week, they might go consecutively through one of the Gospels or follow the lectionary readings for the Christian year. The group leader might choose to use different versions of the Bible, but preference should be given to clear, contemporary translations.

As noted earlier, we may do our meditating in different ways. Some will be more reflective, others more intuitive, and still others more imaginative. Different types of scripture will need different approaches. Meditation on Proverbs will probably rely more on logic than on imagination, whereas meditation on biblical stories invites active imagination. North American adults are probably more skilled in the use of reason than in the use of imagination; they have developed their rational aptitude more than their intuitive or feeling capacities. Consequently, the latter may need special emphasis. It may be helpful to encourage participants to listen to the text like a child who has never heard it before. This kind of listening does not need to conflict with study of scriptures, although some people trained in critical approaches may struggle to use their imaginations. The object of meditation is to go from intellectual processing to letting our inner selves be transformed by the Word.

A fifteen- or twenty-minute period of silence after the reading will give each person time to explore the passage thoroughly. The African-American spiritual "Were You There?" raises the right question. In imagination we put ourselves into the scene. The vast revolution from a more wordy to a more visual culture as a result of recent technological developments may help here. One of my students told me that she was "a more visual person." Are you visually oriented, too, or do you learn better through hearing, reading, or enacting?

In the concluding time when insights are heard, the leader can ask participants, "What jumped out at you? What spoke to your condition?" These are good starters, but people usually don't need much priming. After some minutes of silence, they are ready to let conversation flow. One caution: It is important not to plan an outcome. It is the Word that we want to hear and to which we want to respond.

Example of a Group Meditation

To illustrate, let me give a digest of the sharing from a student group I have led in meditating on the parable of the loving father or the prodigal son (Luke 15:11-32).

Leader: "What jumped out at you? What spoke to your condition?"

a: "The elder brother. I guess I would be more like the brother who stayed home, did everything the father expected, and felt a lot of resentment when the prodigal came home."

L: "What struck you about the elder brother?"

a: "The father's love toward him, notwithstanding his pouting and anger. See, he didn't want to go in, but it says, 'The father went out and urged him.' I've needed to hear that, because I've felt guilty for being angry."

b: "I identified more with the prodigal. I've had a pretty rough life. I didn't have an inheritance to claim, but I cut myself off from my family, just like he did. I couldn't stand my old man. He was always on my back. Never let up, so I got out of there. But I hadn't grown up enough to manage life on my own. I fell in with the wrong crowd—drank like a fish, smoked pot, shacked up with women, and did just as he did. Finally, I hit bottom."

L: "What did you do then?"

b: "I didn't do what the prodigal did. I couldn't go home. Not until after my dad died. But I did find God through AA. You know how that program works, don't you?"

L: "Yes."

c: "What strikes me in this parable is the father's watching and going out. It's in both halves. In the part about the prodigal it says, 'While he was still a long way off, the father saw him.' In that part about the pouty, elder brother, when he refused to come in, it says, 'The father went out and urged him.' That just hit me so hard. That is so unlike what my dad would have done."

L: "It's also unlike a Mid-Eastern father. He had to throw off all dignity."

c: "Well, what does that say about God?"

Mutual sharing about intimate experience of God—when offered freely and not demanded—enables us all to become more fully who we are.

—Norvene Vest

d: "To me it suggests extraordinary love, but it seems a little strange that God would take the initiative in reconciliation. Human parents would want the prodigal to come crawling back and the elder brother to apologize before they accepted them."

L: "I think you have seen the point there. God is not an ordinary parent. God's love is not an ordinary love."

e: "Yeah. If you think about it, you will recognize why God has to take initiative. Physicists now tell us that our universe is made up of more than a hundred fifty billion galaxies. How could we human beings get God's attention if God didn't take the initiative?"

d: "Oh, yes, I see your point. We couldn't shout loud enough, put out a long enough antenna, or send a spaceship far enough to get God's attention if God didn't do that."

f: "As we talk about the parable, it puzzles me that it came to be called 'the parable of the prodigal son.' It's really about the loving father, isn't it?"

L: "Yes, it begins, 'A certain man had two sons.' That's a tip-off."

c: "Right. The father is really the central character who ties both parts of the parable together. I can see now that Jesus was trying to tell us something about God, about the wideness of God's mercy."

a: "I've heard that Jesus told most of his parables in response to critics of his ministry. Whom do you think he was replying to here?"

b: "Probably some of the religious leaders who were critical of his connection with outcasts and sinners like the prodigal."

d: "Oh, that makes it all the more powerful, doesn't it? You can see Jesus confronting those who wanted to claim God only for the respectable. God's love knows no bounds."

L: "Well, that would be a good note to sound for each of us: 'God's love knows no bounds.' Can you hear that word deep inside, confirming what is deepest in you?"

The group meditation would be much more extensive than this summary of high points. However, participants will want some kind of closure. The leader might bring the meditation to a close by having another brief time of silence, reciting the Lord's Prayer, praying a brief verbal prayer, singing a stanza of a familiar hymn, or whatever way would be most appropriate to what has been shared.

Group meditation is another way to feed on the Word of God. It will add to our study of scriptures and listening to God through them. As we use these approaches, however, we keep in mind that our goal is not simply to know the scriptures but to enter into an ever deeper relationship with the living God. May our prayer be like the psalmist's: "As a deer longs for flowing streams, so my soul longs for you, O God. My soul thirsts for God, for the living God" (42:1-2).

DAILY EXERCISES

Read the chapter before you begin the daily exercises. You have learned several different ways to meditate on scripture. This week feel free to use whatever approach feels most comfortable or appropriate as you pray with these stories from the life of Christ. Record your thoughts and experiences in your journal.

EXERCISE 1

Read Mark 3:1-6—Jesus heals a man with a shriveled hand.

EXERCISE 2

Read Luke 13:10-17—Jesus restores a bent-over woman.

EXERCISE 3

Read Mark 6:45-52—Jesus walks on water.

EXERCISE 4

Read John 13:1-17—Jesus washes his disciples' feet.

EXERCISE 5

Read Luke 22:39-46—Jesus prays in Gethsemane.

Remember to review your journal entries for the week in preparation for the group meeting.

Materials for Group Meetings

Informational and Formational Reading

Reading for information is an integral part of teaching and learning. But reading is also concerned with listening for the special guidance, the particular insight, for your relationship with God. What matters is the attitude of mind and heart.

INFORMATIONAL READING

1. Informational reading is concerned with covering as much material as possible and as quickly as possible.

2. Informational reading is linear—seeking an objective meaning, truth, or principle to apply.

3. Informational reading seeks to master the text.

4. In informational reading, the text is an object out there for us to control.

5. Informational reading is analytical, critical, and judgmental.

6. Informational reading is concerned with problem solving.

FORMATIONAL READING

1. Formational reading is concerned with small portions of content rather than quantity.

2. Formational reading focuses on depth and seeks multiple layers of meaning in a single passage.

3. Formational reading allows the text to master the student.

4. Formational reading sees the student as the object to be shaped by the text.

5. Formational reading requires a humble, detached, willing, loving approach to the text.

6. Formational reading is open to mystery. Students come to the scripture to stand before the Mystery called God and to let the Mystery address them.

Adapted from information in *Shaped by the Word: The Power of Scripture in Spiritual Formation* by M. Robert Mulholland Jr. (Nashville, Tenn.: Upper Room Books, 2000), 49–63. Used by permission of Upper Room Books.

The Group Lectio Process

PREPARE

Take a moment to come fully into the present. Sit comfortably alert, close your eyes, and center yourself with breathing.

1. Hear the word (that is addressed to you).
First reading (twice). Listen for the word or phrase from the passage that attracts you. Repeat it over softly to yourself during a one-minute silence. When the leader gives the signal, say aloud only that word or phrase (without elaboration).

2. Ask, "How is my life touched?"
Second-stage reading. Listen to discover how this passage touches your life today. Consider possibilities or receive a sensory impression during the two minutes of silence. When the leader gives the signal, speak a sentence or two, perhaps beginning with the words *I hear, I see, I sense.* (Or you may pass.)

3. Ask, "Is there an invitation here?" (for you).
Third-stage reading. Listen to discover a possible invitation relevant to the next few days. Ponder it during several minutes of silence. When the leader gives the signal, speak of your sense of invitation. (Or you may pass.)

4. Pray (for one another's empowerment to respond).
Pray, aloud or silently, for God to help the person on your right respond to the invitation received.

If desired, group members may share their feelings about the process after completing these steps.

Norvene Vest, *Gathered in the Word: Praying the Scripture in Small Groups* (Nashville, Tenn.: Upper Room Books, 1996), 27. Used by permission of Upper Room Books.

An Annotated Resource List from Upper Room Ministries

*T*he following books relate to and expand on the subject matter of this second volume of *Companions in Christ*. As you read and share with your small group, you may find some material that particularly challenges or helps you. If you wish to pursue individual reading on your own or if your small group wishes to follow up with additional resources, this list may be useful. The Upper Room is the publisher of the books listed, and the number in parentheses is the order number.

1. *Shaped by the Word: The Power of Scripture in Spiritual Formation*, rev. ed., (#936) by M. Robert Mulholland Jr. considers the role of scripture in spiritual formation and challenges you to move beyond informational reading to formational reading of the Bible. Mulholland demonstrates how your approach to scripture will in large measure determine its transforming effect upon your life. He examines the obstacles often faced in opening ourselves to God's living word. You will find this a helpful resource as you examine daily patterns of attentiveness to God through scripture, and you will expand your learnings about formational reading.

2. *Turn Toward Promise: The Prophets and Spiritual Renewal* (#9887) by John Indermark. By reading our daily lives through the prophetic narratives and parables, John Indermark invites us to an energizing spirituality. It is a spirituality that does not shirk the hard demands of justice and peace but realistically asserts that justice and peace have a precondition, namely, the life shaped by trust in God's promises.

3. *A Table of Delight: Feasting with God in the Wilderness* (#9804) by Elizabeth J. Canham. This book invites us to explore the wilderness places in our lives, both the unintended times of barrenness and the chosen "desert times," as opportunities for holy encounter. We can learn

to recognize grace-filled moments when God does provide sustenance in the wilderness of our lives.

4. *Living Out Christ's Love: Selected Writings of Toyohiko Kagawa* (#836). In the period between World Wars I and II, Japanese Christian Toyohiko Kagawa was often mentioned along with Ghandi and Schweitzer as a model of how to blend prayer, personal caring, and social action. Excerpts here include autobiographical reflections and thoughts concerning the Lord's Prayer.

5. *Gathered in the Word: Praying the Scripture in Small Groups* (#806) by Norvene Vest offers detailed guidelines for small groups to engage in a prayerful approach to scripture. The author presents this process in a creative way by giving instructions and then illustrating with a description of a small group that is using this approach to scripture. It is an excellent resource for groups that wish to pray the scriptures together. You were introduced to this group lectio process in the Part 2, Week 5 group meeting.

6. *The Spiritual Formation Bible: Growing in Intimacy with God through Scripture.* This special Bible edition was developed by The Upper Room and published by Zondervan Press. It is available in the NRSV translation. The Bible contains articles on various aspects of spiritual formation and helpful introductions to each book of the Bible. In the margins of the Bible are questions for reflection to guide your prayer and meditation as well as quotations from the spiritual classics.

Continue your exploration of Feeding on the Word by using *Companions in Christ: The Way of Grace* with your small group.

The Way of Grace
By John Indermark, Marjorie Thompson, and Melissa Tidwell
Participant's Book (0-8358-9878-4)
Leader's Guide (0-8358-9879-2)

The Way of Grace invites participants to travel with eight biblical characters (or groups of characters) who discover God's grace through their encounters with Jesus. This resource is more than a survey of the biblical stories in the Gospel of John; it is a transforming interaction with the events and the characters. And it is an invitation for participants to open their hearts to a deeper knowing of God's grace.

Notes

Week 1 Why Do We Call the Bible God's Word?
1. Thomas Merton, *Opening the Bible* (Philadelphia, Pa.: Fortress Press, 1970), 18.
2. M. Robert Mulholland Jr., *Shaped by the Word: The Power of Scripture in Spiritual Formation*, rev. ed. (Nashville, Tenn.: Upper Room Books, 2000), 27, 30.

Week 2 Studying Scripture As a Spiritual Discipline
1. At Qumran the dissidents from the Temple cultus required all who entered the community to take a binding oath to study and abide by the law of Moses (*Manual of Discipline* 5.7–20). They scheduled round-the-clock study for the community.
2. Richard J. Foster, *Celebration of Discipline: The Path to Spiritual Growth*, rev. ed. (San Francisco: Harper & Row, 1988), 62.
3. Thomas Merton, *Spiritual Direction and Meditation* (Collegeville, Minn.: The Liturgical Press, 1960), 44.
4. Ibid., 46.
5. Jean Leclercq, *The Love of Learning and the Desire for God: A Study of Monastic Culture*, trans. Catharine Misrahi (New York: Fordham University Press, 1961), 87–90.

Week 3 Meditating on the Word
1. Merton, *Spiritual Direction and Meditation*, 51.
2. Douglas Burton-Christie, *The Word in the Desert: Scripture and the Quest for Holiness in Early Christian Monasticism* (New York: Oxford University Press, 1993), 107–133.
3. Merton, *Spiritual Direction and Meditation*, 64.
4. Ibid., 95.
5. Elizabeth Canham, unpublished article on *lectio divina*.
6. Merton, *Spiritual Direction and Meditation*, 75.
7. John Cassian, *Conferences* 10.11, trans. Owen Chadwick, The Library of Christian Classics, vol. 12 (Philadelphia: The Westminster Press, 1958), 244.
8. Teresa of Avila, *The Life of Teresa of Jesus, The Autobiography of St. Teresa of Avila*, ed. E. Allison Peers (Garden City, N.Y.: Image Books, 1960), 133.
9. Douglas V. Steere, *Traveling In*, ed. E. Glenn Hinson, Pendle Hill Pamphlet 324 (Wallingford, Pa.: Pendle Hill Publications, 1995), 19.
10. Teresa of Avila, *The Life of Teresa of Jesus*, 137.
11. Bonhoeffer, *Life Together*, trans. John W. Doberstein (New York: Harper & Row, 154), 82.
12. Ibid., 83.
13. Ibid., 84.

Week 4 Directing Imagination
1. Ignatius of Loyola, *The Spiritual Exercises of St. Ignatius*, trans. Anthony Mottola (Garden City, N.Y.: Image Books, 1964), 37.
2. Richard Baxter, *The Saints' Everlasting Rest*, ed. E. Glenn Hinson, The Doubleday Devotional Classics, vol. 1 (Garden City, N.Y.: Doubleday, 1978).
3. John Bunyan, *Grace Abounding* 46, ed. E. Glenn Hinson, The Doubleday Devotional Classics, vol. 1 (Garden City, N.Y.: Doubleday, 1978), 230.

Notes

4. Baxter, *The Saints' Everlasting Rest* 13, 21; 141.
5. Ibid., 14, 2; 142.
6. Quote adapted into modern English idiom from the original text in Richard Baxter, *The Saints' Everlasting Rest* (Philadelphia: Presbyterian Board of Publication, 1847), 306–307.
7. Henri J. M. Nouwen, *Behold the Beauty of the Lord: Praying with Icons* (Notre Dame, Ind.: Ave Maria Press, 1987), 15.

Week 5   Group Meditation with Scripture

1. Bunyan, *Grace Abounding* 77; 237.
2. John Bunyan, *The Pilgrim's Progress*, ed. E. Glenn Hinson, The Doubleday Devotional Classics, vol. 1 (Garden City, N.Y.: Doubleday, 1978), 348.
3. In *A History of Christianity: Readings in the History of the Church*, vol. 2, ed. Clyde L. Manschreck (Englewood Cliffs, N.J.: Prentice-Hall, 1964), 31.
4. Those who would like a more extensive discussion of group meditation will find much help in Norvene Vest's *Gathered in the Word: Praying the Scripture in Small Groups* (Nashville, Tenn.: Upper Room Books, 1996); see especially 17–27.
5. Some may wonder whether the monks did not use primarily the Psalms for *lectio divina*. I believe the answer to that is no. The psalms were chanted in the Opus Dei, the Daily Office monks gathered for eight times a day. During the four hours scheduled for *lectio divina*, they usually meditated on other scriptures and other writings. We probably owe wonderful illuminated manuscripts such as the Lindisfarne Gospels and the Book of Kells to *lectio*.

Sources and Authors
of Margin Quotations

Week 1   Why Do We Call the Bible God's Word?

John Cassian, *Conferences*, Book 14 in *The Spiritual Formation Bible* NRSV (Grand Rapids, Mich.: Zondervan, 1999), n.p.

Thomas à Kempis, *Imitation of Christ* in The *Spiritual Formation Bible* NRSV (Grand Rapids, Mich.: Zondervan, 1999), n.p.

Martin Luther in *The Spiritual Formation Bible* NRSV (Grand Rapids, Mich.: Zondervan, 1999), n.p.

Week 2   Studying Scripture As a Spiritual Discipline

Matthew Henry, *Commentary on the Whole Bible* (27 May 1999) <http://www.ccel.org/h/henry/mhc2/MHC00001.HTM> (21 July 2000), Preface to Volume 1.

Dietrich Bonhoeffer, *Meditating on the Word* (Nashville, Tenn.: The Upper Room, 1986) 44.

Elizabeth J. Canham, *Heart Whispers* (Nashville, Tenn.: Upper Room Books, 1999), 30.

M. Robert Mulholland Jr., *Shaped by the Word* (Nashville, Tenn.: Upper Room Books, 2000), 116.

Week 3   Meditating on the Word

John Calvin, *Golden Booklet of the True Christian Life* (Grand Rapids, Mich.: Baker Book House, 1955), 19.

Richard J. Foster, *Celebration of Discipline* (San Francisco: Harper & Row, 1978), 26.

Norvene Vest, *Gathered in the Word* (Nashville, Tenn.: Upper Room Books, 1996), 11.

John Wesley, *Works*, vol. 14, 253.

Week 4   Directing Imagination

Eugene H. Peterson, *Subversive Spirituality* (Grand Rapids, Mich.: William B. Eerdmans, 1997), 132.

Richard Baxter, *The Saints' Everlasting Rest* (New York: American Tract Society, 1824), 339-340.

Ibid., 349.

John Killinger, *Beginning Prayer* (Nashville, Tenn.: Upper Room Books, 1993), 67.

Avery Brooke, *Finding God in the World* (San Francisco: Harper & Row, 1989), 43.

Week 5   Group Meditation with Scripture

Mary Jean Manninen, *Living the Christian Story* (Grand Rapids, Mich.: William B. Eerdmans, 2000), 6.

Dwight W. Vogel and Linda J. Vogel, (Nashville, Tenn.: Upper Room Books, 1999), *Sacramental Living*, 18.

Norvene Vest, *Gathered in the Word*, (Nashville, Tenn.: Upper Room Books, 1996), 13.

COMPANION SONG
Piano Accompaniment Score

Lyrics by Marjorie Thompson

Music by Dean McIntyre

Optional cut for short version: omit measures 19-34.

Companions in Christ
Part 2 Author

E. Glenn Hinson retired as professor of spirituality and the John Loftis Professor of Church History at Baptist Theological Seminary in Richmond, Virginia, having taught previously at Southern Baptist Theological Seminary. A prolific author and frequent lecturer, Hinson is a member of the *Weavings* Advisory Board, teaches in The Academy for Spiritual Formation, and has written two Upper Room Books, *Love at the Heart of Things* and *Spiritual Preparation for Christian Leadership.*

Journal